Understanding Quality Management Standards

in a week

Michael J. Gilbert

GW00602742

Headway · Hodder & Stoughton

■ A C K N O W L E D G E M E N T S ■

The author and publishers would like to thank the
Department of Trade and Industry for the logo on p. 91.

British Library Cataloguing in Publication Data

A catalogue record for this title is available from the
British Library

ISBN 0 340 618884

First published 1994
Impression number 10 9 8 7 6 5 4 3 2 1
Year   1999 1998 1997 1996 1995 1994

Typeset by Multiplex Techniques Ltd, St Mary Cray, Kent.
Printed in Hong Kong for Hodder & Stoughton Educational,
a division of Hodder Headline Plc, 338 Euston Road, London
NW1 3BH by Colorcraft Ltd.

The Institute of Management (IM) is at the forefront of management development and best management practice. The Institute embraces all levels of management from students to chief executives. It provides a unique portfolio of services for all managers, enabling them to develop skills and achieve management excellence.

For information on the benefits of membership, please contact:

Department HS
Institute of Management
Cottingham Road
Corby
Northants NN17 1TT

Tel. 0536 204222
Fax 0536 201651

This series is commissioned by the Institute of Management Foundation.

C O N T E N T S

Introduction   5

Sunday   What are quality management standards?   6

Monday   Using quality management standards   18

Tuesday   BS 5750: Quality Systems   28

Wednesday   BS 7750: Environmental Management
                 Systems   45

Thursday   BS 7850: Total Quality Management   59

Friday   Planning implementation   73

Saturday   Achieving quality management standards 85

Further reading   95

The impact of quality management standards has been growing significantly since the publication of BS 5750: Quality Systems in 1982.

This has led to the development of quality management standards in the field of Environmental Management (BS 7750) and Total Quality Management (BS 7850). There are continuing developments in national, European and international organisations to encourage the application of quality management standards in ever wider fields of application.

As the terminology of quality management standards becomes part of everyday language in our lives, it is important to understand the underlying concepts. As they provide management with tools and techniques to improve business performance, it is equally important to understand their application.

The objective of this book is to provide an overview of current quality management standards and their application. We shall look at the following:

Sunday	Quality management standards in context
Monday	Standards, processes and application
Tuesday	The requirements of BS 5750
Wednesday	The requirements of BS 7750
Thursday	The guidelines of BS 7850
Friday	Making it happen
Saturday	Assessing the achievement

What are quality management standards?

Today we will look behind quality standards and quality management to get an awareness of the concepts:

- What is quality?
- What are quality management systems?
- What are quality management standards?
- Who writes the standards?
- Its my business!
- Why have standards?

What is quality?

'Quality assured', 'A quality organisation' and 'Quality registered' are now commonplace terms in the market-place used by many companies, but what exactly is meant by quality in this context?

As this book is about standards, we need to look for a definition in a national and international standard: BS 4778/ ISO 8402: Quality Vocabulary states that quality is:

'The totality of features and characteristics of a product or service that bear on its ability to satisfy stated or implied needs.'

The notes that support the definition provide more guidance, and a more commonly used term is 'conformance to the requirements'.

Whatever the customer requirements may be, specified or implied, what we produce should meet those requirements, if it is to be a 'quality' product.

What we produce is controlled by the systems we use to manage the business itself. Only if this management system is right will the finished product 'conform to the requirements'. Quality, therefore is a core management issue, and this integrated business system, designed to ensure we produce or supply 'quality products' is our **quality management system**.

Many customers require assurances that we have satisfactory quality management systems in operation before entering into a contract. It provides evidence of our capability to meet their requirements. But how will they know our quality management system is effective and efficient?

Quality management standards provide a common yardstick against which purchasers can check our quality management system, resulting in 'quality assured' organisations.

What are quality management systems?

Quality management systems encompass all the parts of our organisation that impact on the management of the product quality:

- Our policy on quality (our standards)
- How we are organised (our structure)
- Who does what (roles and responsibilities)
- What things are done (processes and procedures)
- How much effort is required (the resources)
- How we are managed and controlled (the management system)

'Quality' in this context we said is 'conformance to requirements'. It is when a product (like a car) or a service (like a postal delivery) does what it is supposed to do, no more and no less. The car may be a Rolls Royce or Mini, but provided it meets the specified requirements for that car – in terms of reliability, finish, miles per gallon – it can be said to be a quality car. Similarly a postal service that delivers mail accurately and on-time is a quality service, or a journey to work that gets you there easily and economically may be a 'quality' journey.

'Management' is the act (or art) of managing, the way we direct or control resources. In this context resources can be people, equipment, money or a combination of all of these.

We all 'manage' things in our lives, everyday – our time, bank account and journey to work are directed or controlled by ourselves. In work we manage our time, staff, equipment and materials to achieve the objectives we are set.

'Systems' are a series of connected activities that together make a larger whole.

Manufacturing a car is a very complex system with many different activities – designing, modelling, procurement, assembly and testing are just some of them. Your journey to work may involve walking, motoring, public transport or other 'activities'.

The quality management system is a key management responsibility, owned at the highest level in the organisation. The appropriate design of the system is critical to ensure that whatever our policy on quality may be, it is implemented throughout the organisation.

Quality planning and procedures

We may not think a great deal about our journey to work, as long as we get to work on time (meeting that requirement), we just repeat the process the next day. But if our route changes, or we are consistently late, we may have to replan the journey.

Rethinking how we get there, assessing the options available and working out the most promising route is our 'quality plan'.

The more complex a situation, the more we need to write down our quality plan to ensure we get it right, amending it constantly if it proves ineffective. This marks the beginnings of our documented 'controlled process' and 'corrective action' procedures. This is particularly important at work where we are getting things done through other people. Writing things down and communicating the business process to be followed is an essential aspect of quality management systems.

Products

'Product' to most of us means a washing machine or a car; a specific manufactured object. In the world of quality, 'product' means a manufactured product, but *also* any other result of an activity or business process. Therefore, hardware and software, processed material and services, or a combination of any or all of these are all 'products'.

This definition is limited to those things that are intentionally produced, called 'intended products'. This is important when we discuss the environmental management issues, where BS 7750 provides a model to manage 'unintended products', including waste streams, energy use and other by-products.

What are quality management standards?

'Quality management standards' in this context refers to the family of documents that provide the models of quality management system practice for our use.

These models can:

- Help us design, implement and improve our quality management systems
- Act as a yardstick against which to test our quality management systems
- Act as a benchmark to demonstrate to others our competence

We may wish to focus on particular products, on our environmental performance, or on all the functions in the organisation. There are models and guides for each:

- Products and services – BS 5750 (BS/EN/ISO 9000)
- Environmental performance – BS 7750
- Total quality management – BS 7850

An analysis of these three quality management standards will form the core of this book. However, that is not the whole quality standards story.

A family of standards
There is a wide range of subjects covered by the quality standards family which includes:

- Terms used in the quality vocabulary (BS 4778)
- Guidance on audit programmes (BS 7229)
- Models to understand the economics of quality (BS 6143)
- Guidance on designing products (BS 7000)
- Guidance in the preparation of specifications (BS 7373)

Who writes the standards?

British Standards are publications of the British Standards Institution (BSI), the national standards body, incorporated by Royal Charter. The Charter confirms BSI as an independent body, responsible for the production of standards to promote efficiency and harmonisation.

BSI standards committees
All British Standards are prepared by a committee. Each committee has responsibility for making standards in a defined sector or business area, be it chemicals, materials, construction or management.

Committees are made up of expert individuals who are nominated by a relevant interest group from industry, usually through trade associations and similar bodies. The independent chairman is also drawn from industry, appointed by the next senior committee.

The secretary, usually a BSI employee, has to:

- Provide advice and guidance on the standards process, procedures and protocols
- Administer the committee activities, supporting the timetable for the standard development
- Facilitate the process of standard production
- Provide some technical expertise

Consensus
Key to the success of British Standards has been the process of agreement by consensus in committee, which together with a public consultation phase, ensures the contents will meet most users' requirements.

Compliance with British Standards is voluntary, unless it is included in:

- Legislation, (seat belt performance testing)
- Contract requirements (quality management systems conformance)
- Where a claim of compliance has been made

International standards
BSI, as the national standards body, is eligible to participate in European and international standards bodies:

- CEN/CENELEC in Europe
- ISO/IEC at international level

This is important now that 80 per cent of standards work is European or international based. In the next few years there will be continuing developments in European and international quality standards.

Its my business!

We said quality is a management issue and we know there are national and international standards for quality management systems. But how can a remote committee tell us how to run our business?

Quality standards do not tell us how to run our business, they provide guidance on the elements that need to be in place in a quality management system, but *how* we do it is up to us.

To design our own system we have to think about the things that are important in *our business*, we might want to consider:

- Our products and performance – *our purpose*
- Our processes to deliver them – *our systems*
- The expertise required – *our skills*
- The people needed – *our staff*
- The organisation needed to control it – *our structure*
- The values and policies we adopt – *our style*
- The direction we wish to go in – *our strategy*

The interrelation of all these elements will provide *our business* quality management system.

Why have standards?

Standards provide a common yardstick for us all so that we can measure our system's effectiveness using a common basis. Common communication systems benefit us all. In music, the violinist can be Japanese, the orchestra British and the conductor German, but they all work together to produce sounds from a common music annotation system.

This ensures consistency, allows for simplification, and avoids errors and misunderstandings.

There is a 'cost' in developing our understanding, training the people and maintaining the skills, but these costs are outweighed by the gains. Like learning music, learning 'quality' is both challenging and rewarding.

Types of standard
There are different types of standard for different uses:

Guides provide recommendations on things that *should* be done to achieve an end result, e.g. BS 7850 or BS 5750: Part 8.

Specifications are more demanding, stating what must or *shall* be done to comply with a standard, e.g. BS 7750 or BS/EN/ISO 9001.

Systems assessment
Specifications allow formal assessments or audits of compliance with the standard to take place. Audits can be:

- Internal for our own information (first party)
- External by a customer for their own use (second party)
- External by an independent body (third party)

This latter route is used by many organisations to simplify and reduce the costs of many and varied second party audits.

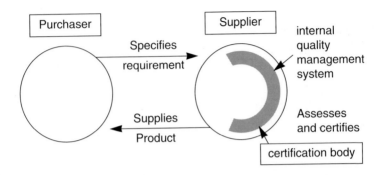

A quality audit is defined as:

'A systematic, independent examination to determine whether quality activities and related results comply with the planned arrangements, and whether these arrangements are implemented effectively and are suitable to achieve objectives.' (BS 4778)

This indicates the extent to which the audit examines the system and looks at:

- What we say we do
- What is being done
- How well is it being done
- The results achieved
- Whether we are doing the right things

We will look at audits again on Friday.

Summary

- Quality is about ensuring that our output or performance meets the requirements we need
- Quality standards are an indicator of 'best practice' agreed by a national or international groups of experts
- Quality management standards provide yardsticks of good management practice anyone can use
- The quality management system is our system owned by our management
- Using the standards can provide assurance to ourselves and others of our capability to meet policy and performance objectives
- Compliance with quality management standards can be objectively assessed

Using quality management standards

On Sunday, we established that quality management standards provide models of good management practice, without telling us how to run our business. Today we will explore the principle elements of such models including:

- Quality management system design
- Quality management system organisation
- Quality management system planning
- Implementation
- Model selection

Quality management system design

In order to design a quality management system we must understand how things happen in organisations. Breaking down the whole into parts will allow us to see how it all fits together.

The basic building block is the 'business process', defined in the TQM standard BS 7850, as an activity that accepts an 'input' of some kind, adds value through doing something and produces an 'output'. The process will require some resources to operate, people or machinery, and will need some form of management control.

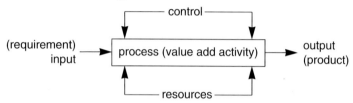

In order to ensure the output, or product, meets the requirements, we need to understand what is wanted. This can be a process in itself, with the output a set of requirements, which might be in the form of a specification.

In addition, other people have to produce the product, package it, store it and deliver it. Many interdependent processes exist in the organisation, and a simple chain might look like this.

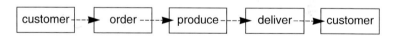

This seems straightforward. Yet there are a lot of business activities missing in this simple process.

What about the suppliers we use? Who designs the product? Who is checking that we are producing the things on time, within budget, to the right specification? Who is checking we are operating legally and complying with our own internal policies?

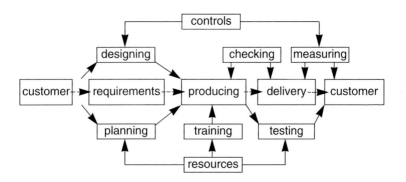

Each department or business process can be examined against this model. Questions, such as 'Who is the 'customer' for our output?' 'What do they want?' and, 'How do we know we are doing the right things the right way?' need to be asked.

The 'customer' might be:

- An external organisation
- Another internal department
- A corporate policy
- A legal requirement

Quality management system organisation

All of these activities and processes may be organised within our business in traditional layers, to balance responsibility and authority, each layer having different objectives within the organisation.

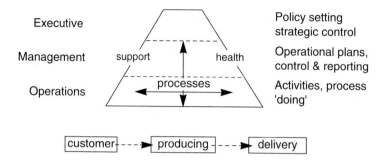

Executive management provide the business strategic direction, make decisions on policies, goals, resource levels, products, expansion or contraction. They need accurate and timely information to make appropriate decisions.

Management implement the strategic decisions and policies, direct and control operational resources, collate information and advise on problems and opportunities. They need clear guidelines within which to operate, and appropriate skills, resources and authority to be effective.

Operations carry out the day-to-day activities and business processes, reporting progress, achievements, and issues for resolution.

In addition there will be resources identified to support the business as it changes and check its 'health'.

Within each of these layers, business processes exist: at the highest level, a strategic business planning process; at the middle level, a departmental control process, and at the operational level, procurement, production and delivery processes. Organising them into an effective coordinated operation requires planning.

Quality management system planning

In order to ensure success, the executive, managerial and operational elements of our organisation must fit together. There should be no gaps which might leave things undone, and there should be no overlap to ensure we do not waste resources and cause confusion.

We are trying to ensure that:

- We satisfy the recipient of the process (the customer) at optimum cost to the organisation, using our resources effectively
- We satisfy our customer to maintain his confidence in our ability as a supplier

This is common sense, and the elements that need to be present in our quality management system will be just that – common sense. There will be management practices based on what we need to get right, and what we can't afford to get wrong. The critical areas might be any of the following:

Product image	Market share
Design standards	Product performance
Production control	Pollution
Staff skills	Resource costs
Competition	Changing markets
Storage or delivery	Supplier continuity
Raw materials	Regulatory climate
Disposal issues	Stakeholder issues

We need to look at each area where a critical factor could affect our success, then establish a business process to provide a method of reducing that risk.

Areas of risk

Staff may not understand the importance of customer requirements being met

Tell them about our policy on customer satisfaction

Staff may not understand their jobs

Tell them what the job is about and the performance required

Staff may not have the skills or resources to do their jobs effectively

Analyse the skills and resources needed and provide for them in the business plans

Staff may not understand how the process is meant to operate

Describe the processes in a clear way to ensure understanding

Staff may not follow what has to be done

Check that work is completed correctly

The processes may be incomplete or overlap

Set out and review plans of the quality system and business processes

We may not be able to do what the customer wants

Check that the requirements can be met

Our suppliers may let us down
Establish a supplier checking system
Production may not be set up correctly to achieve the standards required
Review and document the procedures to ensure they comply
Defects may occur in production – obvious ones, and hidden ones
Establish testing and measurement systems, including special tests for 'hidden' problems
Test equipment could give the wrong readings
Set up a method to check test equipment
The management system may be incomplete or ineffective
We must assess the system's completeness and performance

If we take each of these processes or activities we can then see the beginnings of a picture or model of what processes need to be in place in our organisation for us to ensure our product will meet the customer requirements. For each element we need to write down what should happen and then follow through and do it.

Implementation

Having established the process, it is important to follow it, otherwise the system is ineffective.

No system is perfect, if we find that we need to do things differently, then we must change the written process to align with what is done. If we find we need to design the business process differently, we must document the new approach and change what we do.

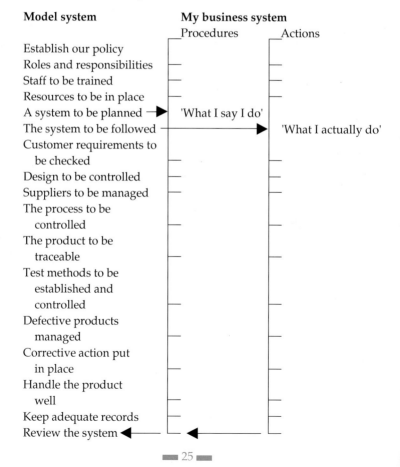

Model system

My business system
Procedures   Actions

Establish our policy
Roles and responsibilities
Staff to be trained
Resources to be in place
A system to be planned → 'What I say I do'
The system to be followed → 'What I actually do'
Customer requirements to be checked
Design to be controlled
Suppliers to be managed
The process to be controlled
The product to be traceable
Test methods to be established and controlled
Defective products managed
Corrective action put in place
Handle the product well
Keep adequate records
Review the system ◀

Model selection

Quality systems
On Tuesday, we examine BS 5750: Quality Systems, for use where a purchaser requires assurance from a supplier of his capability to supply a product or service.

Environmental management systems
We examine the detailed requirements of BS 7750 on Wednesday, but the key difference in understanding the use of this standard is the 'customer requirement' element in the system.

If we wish to assure ourselves and others that our environmental policies and performance meet requirements, then we may follow the quality management system concept, but we need to define the requirements in a different way. Expectations of environmental performance may come from legislators, shareholders, staff or the general community. We have to translate the expectations into targets of performance, which are specifications for environmental performance.

To do this we need to understand the environmental effects of our organisation and set targets to change these effects over time. As part of our environmental improvement programme, an environmental effects analysis process is required.

Total quality management (TQM)
BS 7850 provides guidance to the application of total quality management. As this is only guidance, compliance cannot

be assessed against a set of specific criteria. The documents indicate principles and methods to follow in applying TQM concepts in an organisation.

Summary

We spent Monday considering the use of quality system standards and looked at:

- System design through consideration of our activities
- The management infrastructure that needs to be in place to direct and control the system
- System planning, looking at our customer needs and internal efficiencies
- Analysing system elements by looking at the things that may go wrong
- Application of quality standards to address environmental and TQM requirements

BS 5750: Quality Systems

On Sunday and Monday, we explored quality management standards in general and how the use of them could make our organisation more efficient and effective. Today, we will look at the first model for a quality system: BS/EN/ISO 9001: Quality Systems – model for quality assurance in design, development, production, installation and servicing.

Background

This standard was first published in 1979, later revised in 1987 as a European (EN 29000) and international (ISO 9000) standard. It has recently been revised again as BS/EN/ISO 9001: 1994.

There are five standards to the BS/EN/ISO 9000 series:

- ISO 9000 – 1: Quality management and quality assurance standards
    - Part 0: Principles concepts and applications
    - Part 1: Guide to selection and use

This standard provides a background to the concepts, and details the characteristics of quality system application and the choice of 'model' available to use as an appropriate yardstick.

- BS/EN/ISO 9001: Quality Systems – model for quality assurance in design, development, production, installation and servicing

This standard specifies the system requirements for all stages in product provision, from design through to servicing.

- BS/EN/ISO 9002: Quality Systems – model for quality assurance in production and installation

This standard specifies the system requirements for all stages of product provision from production to servicing, but excludes design.

- BS/EN/ISO 9003: Quality Systems – model for quality assurance in final inspection and test

This standard specifies the system requirements for the inspection and testing of finished products against predetermined criteria.

- BS/EN/ISO 9004: Quality management and quality system elements – guidelines

This standard provides general guidance on quality management and quality systems. Its contents include:

Interests and expectations	Personnel training and motivation
Specification and design quality	Economics of quality systems
Production quality and control	Procurement quality
Product verification	Marketing quality
Control of measuring and test equipment	Nonconformity
Handling and post production	Corrective and preventive action
Quality documentation and records	Product safety and reliability
	Statistical methods

This standard is a general text that helps us to understand the quality system requirements specified in BS/EN/ISO 9001, and should be read *before* the model to give the background.

BS/EN/ISO 9001: Quality Systems

This will be explored in depth as it is the key quality systems specification. It has a national *foreword* which indicates the formal link to the international series, the 1987 version and the European standard.

The *introduction* (clause 0) refers to the complementary applications of ISO 9001/2/3 and their intention to provide models for a supplier of products to demonstrate capability, providing a yardstick for external assessment.

It notes that the quality system standard is not alternative to the product specification but complementary – covering the systematic approach required to achieve success in meeting the specified product requirements. It emphasises that the solution adopted must be tailored to meet the needs of a specific business.

The diagram below shows the purchaser/supplier relationship discussed on Monday expanded to relate to the BS/EN/ISO 9001 requirements.

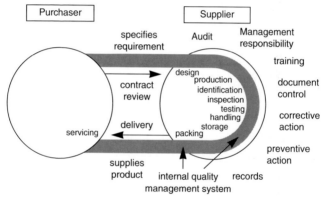

The *scope* (1) defines the application of the standard, i.e. where our ability to design and supply products that conform to requirements needs to be demonstrated. Achieving customer satisfaction through the prevention of nonconformity in all stages of our activities.

Other standards that are applicable within the context of this standard are called *normative references* (2), e.g. ISO 8042: Quality Vocabulary.

The *definitions* (3) also refer to ISO 8042 and include another term – product. This sets an important concept of product. As we saw on Sunday the result of our activities is a 'product', including services, hardware, software, processed material or any combination of these.

The *quality system requirements* (4) are stated in 20 sub-clauses.

The *management responsibilities* (4.1) include setting out the quality policy, which must:

- Be defined by executive management and written down
- Set objectives and commitment to achieving them
- Be relevant to our goals and our customer expectations
- Be understood, implemented and maintained throughout our organisation

We need to define and document the responsibility and authority of our staff whose work affects the quality of our product, especially those who need to:

- Take action to stop things going wrong
- Examine quality problems that have occurred
- Take action to resolve those problems
- Check solutions are in place and control is maintained to ensure that problems are resolved

We must assess and allocate the right levels of resources, including competent people in key areas:

- In management
- Carrying out work activities
- Checking work is properly done
- Assessing the systems conformance

There must be a management representative, whose job is to ensure the requirements of the standard are met. He/she reports on the system's performance through a management review as a basis for planning improvements.

The management review is a regular, recorded assessment by our executive team of our system's adequacy and effectiveness in meeting the standard and implementing our policy and objectives.

Under the *quality system* (4.2) requirements there is a general need to set up, document and operate a quality management system. The outline structure of the system will be recorded in a manual with references to the standard.

Documented quality system procedures will be set up to implement our policy. The procedures must then be implemented to meet the requirements of the standard. The degree to which we have to document everything will vary with the activities involved, the skills needed and the skills people acquire doing the job.

Our documentation must define our quality planning activities, including:

- Consistency with our other business practices and procedures
- Preparing a plan to achieve the quality required
- Identifying and acquiring the skills and resources needed
- Making sure the processes from design through production installation and testing are integrated
- Testing and inspection methods are current

- Developing new ways to measure and verify conformance
- Establishing the standards to be met at key stages
- The records we plan to keep to demonstrate conformance

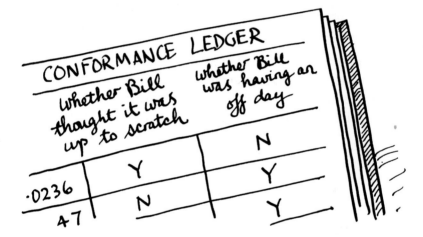

Under *contract review* (4.3) there is a general need to establish and maintain procedures to review and record every contract we accept to make sure:

- The requirements we have to meet are suitably clear and recorded
- Any differences between our tender and the order are cleared up
- We can meet the requirements specified

We must also establish a method to make amendments to a contract after it is let and how relevant departments will know.

We need to maintain *design control* (4.4) to ensure the design of the product will meet the requirements agreed in the contract review. The design procedures include:

- Design and development planning, describing methods and ownership by suitably qualified people
- Where other people have organisational and technical interfaces with the design activities, we must define the relationships and ensure that current information is available at all times
- Where other design input requirements have to be considered, including legal requirements, we must ensure they are adequately defined and accurate. Where there are anomalies in this information, these must be resolved with those imposing the requirements
- As the design progresses, we need to plan, hold and record design reviews. Present at the reviews will be all relevant personnel
- Design output must be expressed in terms that:
  - meet the specified requirement
  - refer to the acceptance criteria or standards
  - describe the characteristics that are key to safety and effective functioning of the product
  These documents must be reviewed before release
- Design verification will take place, and be recorded, at various stages to ensure the design can move on to the next stage
- Design validation will be used to test that the product in use conforms to the requirements and user needs
- As the design progresses, all design changes will be properly authorised and documented by qualified staff

Notes explain that design validation follows verification and is usually performed on the final product in use.

We have to put in place methods for *document and data control* (4.5). Document approval and issue procedures must exist to:

- Ensure documents are reviewed and approved before issue by authorised staff
- Keep a master schedule readily available showing the documents and their status so people do not use out-of-date documents
- Keep current documents where they are needed
- Ensure that invalid or superseded documents are removed or properly handled to avoid incorrect use
- Ensure that superseded documents that need to be kept for record purposes are properly identified

We also need to make sure that document changes are carried out by the same staff that issued the original, unless designated otherwise. The designated staff must have access to relevant background material for the review and update process. Changes to documents must be identified.

We must put in place written *purchasing* (4.6) controls to ensure we get from our suppliers products that meet our specified requirements. These controls should include:

- Carrying out evaluation of subcontractors to ensure that they are chosen on the basis of their ability to meet our requirements

- Directing the subcontractor, dependent on his demonstrated capability and significance of the impact of the subcontractor on the final product quality
- Keeping records of acceptable subcontractors

Orders placed with our subcontractors must have adequate purchasing data to cover:

- What we want – the specific product
- How we want it – inspection methods or approval process
- The applicable quality system standard

When considering verification of the purchased product we may check at our subcontractor's premises, and must specify how in the purchasing documents.

Our customer may specify that he wants to check a subcontractor's product. However these checks by the customer do not take away our responsibility to ensure we provide satisfactory products.

Where we are responsible for the *control of customer supplied product* (4.7) to be incorporated into our product, we must:

- Have a written system to check and look after the product
- Report any lost, damaged or unfit items

Where required we will need to establish methods of *product identification and traceability* (4.8) to cover:

- The product from the start to the end of our process
- The product or batch after it leaves us with a unique identification
- Maintain records of the product identification

Process control (4.9) is required for those of our production, installation and servicing activities that affect the quality of the final product. These must be carried out under 'controlled conditions' and include:

- Written methods, where their lack could result in defects
- The use of suitable equipment in an appropriate working environment
- Complying with written standards or methods
- Tracking and controlling activities and results against preset parameters
- Clear standards of workmanship through illustration or samples
- Regular maintenance of equipment to avoid failure

Where the output from a process cannot be checked until the product is in use, we may need to take special steps, for example, pre-qualifying the process, then using qualified operators and continual monitoring and control. Also, maintenance of records of the standards achieved should be followed.

We must establish adequate *inspection and testing* (4.10) methods to ensure the product meets requirements, and keep records to demonstrate that compliance.

When receiving supplies we must not use them until satisfied they meet our requirements. This checking will include consideration of the verification activities of our subcontractors.

If, for reasons of urgency, we do use supplies before checking, we need to identify when this has happened so as to be able to take action in the event of a problem, e.g. recall and replace.

When the product is in process we must follow our quality plan for testing, not releasing to the next stage unless the tests are complete, except where we have a positive recall procedure.

The final inspection and testing activities include:

- Those designated in the quality plan to demonstrate conformance to requirements
- Verification that all receiving and in-process tests are complete and satisfactory
- Holding the product until all information is available and authorised

The inspection and test records must show:

- The steps taken
- The pass/fail records
- The method of controlling the non-conforming product
- Release authorisation records

We need to establish *control of inspection, measuring and test equipment* (4.11) through written methods, to ensure it is able to provide the required measurement certainty. Such methods will include checking that software and hardware provide the measurement accuracy required and is regularly checked. This information must be made available to the customer if he/she requires it.

The control procedure requires that we:

- Decide the measurement accuracy we want and put in place equipment to meet that need
- Schedule all the test equipment and calibrate it to written standards at set times

- Specify the calibration protocol to be followed, and the acceptance criteria and actions if the results show problems
- Mark equipment to show its calibration status
- If we find out-of-calibration problems, check the implications on previous results using the equipment
- Make sure the environmental conditions are right for the calibration and testing activities
- Handle, store and keep the equipment to ensure it is accurate

Having established test methods and accuracy, we need to track the *inspection and test status* (4.12) of the product so that we know it has met the required criteria at any stage in the process. No product must be released unless it has passed the tests or is released under a concession.

We must have adequate *control of nonconforming product* (4.13) to ensure it is not accidentally used.

Where a problem has been identified, we need to define authority for nonconforming product review and disposition. The review has to decide whether to: rework; accept with or without repair by concession; regrade for other use, or reject and scrap.

We must ask for a concession if we plan to use non-conforming or repaired products under the contract, documenting the actual condition. Repaired or reworked products must go back through our inspection procedures.

We need to put in place methods to carry out *corrective and preventive action* (4.14) to eliminate problems. The actions we take need to be related to the size of the problems and the risks anticipated. When we change the process as a result, we need to record what has been done.

Our methods for corrective action must include:

- Handling defect reports and complaints
- Noting the results of investigations into problems
- Deciding what course of action to take
- Completing the action and ensuring it is effective

Our methods for preventive action must include: using a wide range of information sources to identify potential causes of defects; identifying the actions needed to eliminate the risk; implementing the changes and reviewing them.

We need to set up and operate written methods of *handling, storage, packaging and delivery* (4.15) of our products. Our methods of handling must prevent damage or deterioration. Storage needs to be in defined areas and appropriate ways of controlling what goes in and out established, together with checks to monitor deterioration.

We must package our products appropriately and have a method of preserving them while under our control, including adequate protection up to and including delivery.

We have to set up and operate a method for keeping *control of quality records* (4.16). The records need to be arranged in such a way that they are readily accessible, over a defined period of time, and are able to show that:

- Our products conform to specified requirements
- Our quality system operates effectively

Our subcontractor's records will be part of this information.

We need to set up and operate methods to plan and carry out *internal quality audits* (4.17) to ensure that:

- We have appropriate procedures in place
- They are being followed
- The result is products that conform to requirements

Auditing must be planned, focused on the important activities first, and carried out by people who are independent of the area being assessed. The manager of the assessed area must be advised of defects and take action to correct those found.

We must keep records of the audits, results and subsequent actions to show that problems are corrected.

We must provide adequate *training* (4.18), so we need to operate written procedures to: identify training needs; provide training and keep records. It is essential to ensure that all key staff are qualified on the basis of education, training or experience.

If we are required to provide *servicing* (4.19) then we need to have appropriate written methods to carry this out.

We must establish what *statistical techniques* (4.20) we need in order to ensure our processes will create the product characteristics we want. Having identified the need we must then set up and operate procedures to carry out and control the application of these techniques.

Summary

Today we have explored the BS/EN/ISO 9000 series:

- Five parts provided three specifications and two guides for the application of quality systems in any organisation
- BS/EN/ISO 9000 provides guidance on the selection and use of the models or specifications. The specifications can be used with some omissions to suit particular activities
- BS/EN/ISO 9001/2/3 are specifications for use related to the scope of our activities; from design right through to installation; production to installation; or just inspection and testing
- The specification requires us to set up, operate and maintain a series of documented methods or processes to reflect what needs to be done to produce products that meet specified requirements – the quality system
- The system assessment focuses on what we say we do, compared to what we actually do, and how effective it is in achieving products that meet the specified requirements

BS 7750: Environmental Management Systems

Today, we examine the standard with similar quality management principles, but a different focus: BS 7750: 1994: Specification for environmental management systems. This standard was first published in 1992 and was revised in 1994 following experience in use.

The standard

BS 7750 has four parts:

- Foreword
- The requirements
- Annex A – Guide to environmental management system requirements
- Annex B – Links to BS 5750 Quality Systems

Foreword
The foreword links a number of related issues to 'position' the standard:

1 It specifies an EMS that can be used to satisfy ourselves and others that we meet environmental policies and objectives that we have publicly committed to.
2 The EMS provides a foundation for environmental auditing.
3 The EMS is designed to be integrated into existing management systems, varying some components.

4 BS 7750 has links to BS 5750 so that organisations whose existing quality management systems comply may achieve equivalence with BS 7750 using an appropriate industry sector application guide.

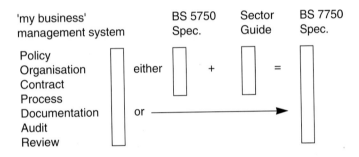

5 Assessment may be part of existing audit programmes providing the audit team has:

- Appropriate environmental skills
- Detailed knowledge of the requirements of BS 7750

6 The requirements are designed to be compatible with the EU Eco-management and audit regulation (EMA), (with the exception of the need to publish a verified environmental statement).

7 It indicates that accreditation and certification will be available during 1994.

8 There is a 'health warning' that the standard does not establish standards for environmental performance, other than compliance with legislation and to continually improve, e.g. two similar organisations, with different environmental performance standards, may still comply.

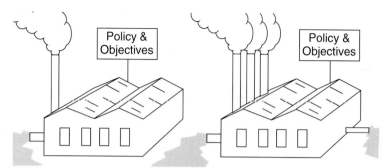

9 Sector application guides have a role to play in identifying environmental effects or performance standards for industrial sectors where environmental issues are complex.

10 There is a reference to the contribution of the pilot programme participants in the development of the standard.

The specification

The introduction sets the standard in the context of environmental performance issues, legislation and environmental auditing activities. It confirms the need for a structured management system which will give confidence that appropriate environmental performance criteria are established and met within our organisation.

The generic nature of the standard is highlighted and a 'route map' for implementation suggested (see diagram).

It is noted that the standard is intended to support certification schemes.

The guide (Annex A) and links to BS 5750 (Annex B) are introduced, and it is noted that conformance with BS 5750 is helpful, but not a prerequisite to compliance with BS 7750.

Items in **bold** form the specification.

The specification confirms the compatible but independent status of BS 7750 which allows separate assessment and certification if required by an organisation.

The scope (1.0) defines the scope of the specification, which, if applied, will ensure we comply with our stated environmental policy and objectives, and enable us to demonstrate that compliance.

Informative references (2.0) indicate standards and other documents that provide additional information relevant to this standard:

- BS 5750: Quality systems
- BS 7729: Quality systems auditing
- EU Eco-management and audit regulation 1993
- Environmental Protection Act 1990

Definitions (3) establish the meaning adopted for particular words and phrases used throughout the standard.

The requirements

The *environmental management systems requirements* (4) are stated in eleven sub-clauses that form the core specification requirements to be followed for compliance.

A *general* (4.1) clause requires us to set up and operate an EMS to ensure that our environmental effects conform to policy, objectives and targets. It tells us we must establish a written system and implement it.

Clause 4.2 *environmental policy* says we must write down our policy, ensuring it is:

- Relevant to what we do and the effects of our activities on the environment
- Communicated and made effective throughout the organisation
- Made available to the public, together with any environmental objectives that are related to it
- Comprehensive in describing which of our activities are covered by the system

Organisation and personnel establishes the requirement for a well-defined organisational structure.

We need to identify the *responsibility, authority and resources* so that the relationships of people whose work has an environmental effect are defined and written down. This includes those who need to:

- Appoint staff and manage resources
- Take action to implement policy
- Examine and track environmental problems
- Take action to solve those problems
- Act in an emergency situation

We need to put in place *verification resources and personnel* to confirm our compliance with the requirements of the standard, and use skilled people in a structured way.

A *management representative* must be appointed with responsibility to ensure we meet the standard.

We need to set up ways to manage *personnel, communication and training* issues, particularly:

- How important it is to comply with our environmental policy and meet the requirements of BS 7750
- How important people's work is in relation to complying with our policy
- The benefits of continual improvements in environmental performance
- The problems that could arise if things go wrong through not following the procedures
- The need to identify and satisfy EMS training needs
- The need to ensure the training is effective and recorded

We also need to set up a method to ensure that our subcontractors are aware of our EMS requirements.

Clause 4.4 *environmental effects,* indicates the need to understand how we affect the environment by examining three key areas.

Communications from all those people with an interest in our environmental effects must be managed. Therefore we need to set up and operate a method to receive, administer and respond to anyone with a relevant interest. These may include statutory bodies, local authorities, neighbours, staff, pressure groups, investors, customers or the general public.

Second, we need to implement an *environmental effects evaluation and register* system. Its purpose is to list the significant issues, actual or potential that relate to all our activities, including:

- Emissions to air, discharges to water and other wastes, planned or unplanned
- Land that is, or may be, contaminated
- Resources and how we use them, including land, water, energy etc
- Other impacts in the form of noise, smells, dust, the appearance of our buildings
- Unusual activities e.g. starting up/shutting down plant
- Accidental occurrences, incidents and potential emergency situations
- Historic activities and future plans

Third, we need to implement a system to establish a register of *legislative, regulatory and other policy requirements*. This will include any codes of practice or standards that are relevant to all our activities.

These three parts prepare us to put in place *environmental objectives and targets* (4.5) at all levels in the organisation. This process will need to take into account, and be consistent with:

- The environmental effects
- Our environmental policy
- Other business needs, financial and commercial

In order for the objectives and targets to be meaningful, we are required to quantify them, and to show our commitment to continual improvement over time.

Having set the objectives and targets across the organisation, we need collate these into an *environmental management programme* (4.6) to show how we plan to achieve them. The plan will need to show:

- Who is responsible for achieving the objectives and targets
- How they will go about achieving them, including identifying the resources needed

Where we have new projects or significant changes in our existing working methods, we need to make sure that environmental objectives are also established.

Having laid out the programme we need to document key elements. *Environmental management manual and documentation* (4.7) specifies the requirements:

- The policy, objectives, targets and programme
- Identification of the ownership of parts of the programme

- The links between the various parts of the EMS; the link to the business management system and other related documentation

The manual must also include consideration of any out-of-the-ordinary events, accidents and emergency situations and how we might deal with them.

The manual, together with other related documentation, needs to be properly managed to be useful and effective. We need to set up and operate a system to ensure:

- Documents exist where they are needed
- Each document is identified with a relevant part of the organisation or activity
- They are owned, reviewed, updated and approved by staff with appropriate authority
- Superseded documents are not used

The documentation can be paper or electronic based, but it must be readily understood and it must be clear what the current versions are. We should identify what documents have to be kept and for how long.

We need to make sure that work identified as relevant to our significant environmental effects is effectively managed through *operational control* (4.8).

This means making sure that managers' responsibilities are clear and that written control, measurement and checking activities are properly integrated and working, particularly:

- Where there is a risk of breaching our policy
- Where subcontractors do work on our behalf
- To ensure that inputs, outputs, wastes and resources are tracked and actual performance checked

We will need verification of our actual performance to meet this last point, and therefore will need to:

- Decide what information we want and the accuracy required
- Decide the methods for obtaining the data and the measurement technique
- Set up and operate the methods to generate the records we need
- Decide what we will do if the records show problems in our operations
- Make sure our measurement equipment is accurate

Where problems are identified, we need to set up and operate non-compliance and corrective actions to ensure that:

- Responsibility and authority is defined
- The way of investigating and correcting problems is clear so that we can:

- identify the root cause
- plan and implement changes to solve the problem
- record what happened

Environmental management records (4.9) are required to show that the EMS is:

- Being followed
- Effective and that the targets are being met

To do that, the records must be:

- Properly identified, managed and maintained
- Accessible and readable
- Retained as planned and appropriately disposed

The documents and records provide the basis for our *environmental management audits* (4.10) the process by which we check the 'health' of our EMS. The requirements include:

- Setting up and operating audit procedures and programmes
- Checking if our actions comply with our environmental plans
- That the results meet our targets and objectives

The audit programme must cover:

- What areas are to be assessed and when
- Who is responsible for initiating the audit

The *audit protocols and procedures* (4.10) define how the audit
will be done, and specify:

- The documents to be examined
- The actual environmental performance to be
  examined
- The personnel involved (who must be independent
  and competent)
- How the assessment will be done and the results
  reported
- The programme for correcting non-compliance
  issues

Finally we need to carry out documented *environmental
management reviews* (4.11) to ensure that the EMS:

- Meets the requirements of BS 7750
- Fits our needs and is working
- Is changed if required

This concludes the specification requirements.

The Annexes

The Annexes provide additional information relevant to the specification. They are not meant to add requirements, but to explain and clarify.

Annex A
This follows the specification layout so that each clause has a matching Annex section focused on that topic.

The *specification clause* 4.1 states 'The organisation shall establish and maintain an environmental management system...'

The Annex clause A4 states 'the environmental management system components will be inextricably woven through most, if not all of the organisation's overall management system.'

The annex therefore broadens understanding and will be essential reading for our managers and staff when we embark on our programme.

The only clause in Annex A not directly related to the specification clauses is A.1.2, *preparatory environmental review*. This, referred to in the introduction, is a useful first step to assess our current environmental performance.

This is an activity we would initiate before implementing an EMS to provide our baseline.

Annex B
This provides links to BS 5750 for organisations whose management system is assessed against that standard. This will allow us to ensure that broader requirements arising

from BS 7750 are incorporated into our integrated management system.

Summary

Today, we explored the environmental management system standard, BS 7750, which is a single document containing introductory information, a specification and guidance on the application of quality management concepts to environmental performance.

- The specification states the elements essential for an effective environmental management system in any organisation
- Compliance requires specific practices, procedures and methods to assess our environmental performance; establish policy; document our effects; set up objectives and targets, control implementation procedures; audit and review our achievements
- Guidance is included in the document to help us implement our EMS and integrate it into our management system if it is related to BS 5750

BS 7850: Total Quality Management

Over the last two days we have examined standards that establish performance requirements through specifications.

The standard we review today provides guidance to the subject and therefore compliance is not directly assessable. The standard establishes important principles and concepts that, when used within an organisation, enhance and improve the quality management beyond the product or environmental performance to a comprehensive, embracing 'total' quality culture.

The standard was published in 1992 in two parts:

- BS 7850: Total quality management
  - Part 1: Guide to management principles
  - Part 2: Guide to quality improvement methods

BS 7850: Part 1

This part is designed to provide guidance to our senior management on the application of the principles involved in improving organisational effectiveness, it is laid out as:

- A foreword
- A guide including:
  - fundamental concepts
  - implementing TQM
  - role of supporting techniques
- Informative Annexes
  - A Examples of a typical process of TQM
  - B Example of a systematic improvement process

The foreword
This sets the scene for the guide, lays out the relationship of the two parts, and introduces the TQM concept of aligning every part of our business activities to ensure maximum effectiveness and efficiency.

It also confirms the interrelationship of various objectives that have to be met by our organisation:

- Customer satisfaction
- Health and safety
- Environmental objectives
- Business goals

These objectives underline that the key investment to be made is in training people in new ways of doing things. It will also take quite a while to change our organisation into

an integrated business unit with a single management goal –
to satisfy all requirements effectively and efficiently across
the whole organisation.

The guide
The *introduction* reinforces the concept of organisational
objectives, including the key one of 'customer satisfaction',
being cascaded to all staff. To develop the harmonisation of
effort towards these goals, full participation and leadership
from management is essential within a continual
improvement culture.

The importance of measuring current performance is
emphasised, and the need for appropriate management
tools to identify and help correct inbuilt and repetitive
(chronic) problems in our organisations operations is made
explicit.

The *scope* (1.0) clarifies that Part 1 focuses on the
management principles for meeting objectives in an effective
way through the use of TQM implementation.

The *reference* (2.0) clause links sources that need to be read in conjunction with this standard (normative):

- BS 4778: Quality vocabulary
- BS 6143: Process cost model
- BS 7850: Part 2

as well as sources that could be read to provide further information (informative):

- BS 5750: quality systems

The *definitions* (3.0) cover the key words and phrases not included in the quality vocabulary in BS 4778.

The definition of the key concept of business 'process' is that it describes activities that have an input, add value and produce output received by a customer.

The 'process owner' is the person responsible for the activities. This person is also a 'customer' receiving input and a 'supplier' providing output.

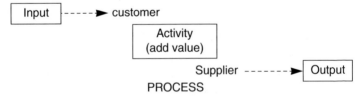

The *fundamental concepts* (4.0) can be summarised in eleven sub sections:

1 General guidance that all the elements are required for TQM.
2 Commitment is required at the top of the organisation, with everyone below that involved.

3 Customer satisfaction is key and everyone has a customer.

4 Quality losses occur in any organisation due to failure to use resources effectively.

5 Participation by all is necessary.

6 Process measurement will be applied throughout the organisation.

7 Continuous improvement will be sought.

8 Problem identification will be used to focus on inhibitors to process improvement.

9 Alignment of corporate objectives and individual attitudes will help remove existing prejudices.

10 Personal accountability will be recognised to be accepted by all, which demands that:

11 Personal development becomes a feature of the organisation.

Implementing total quality management (5.0) has six parts covering the following:

- A general focus on implementation through cascading a quality systems approach, tools and techniques (Annex A)
- Creating appropriate organisational structures and the rewards and procedures to meet the new needs
- Implementing process management concepts to establish the purpose, inputs, outputs, ownership, standards and measurements applied to all the business processes
- How the measurement of performance will change towards objective, data-based systems, agreed between business process owners and customers

- Introducing improvement planning techniques to ensure quality improvement is planned, implemented, analysed and replanned
- Training required in all aspects of TQM for all staff

The *role of supporting techniques* (6.0) is covered in three sections:

- Quality systems focus on the need for a management system to be in place to ensure the business process outputs meet requirements
- Quality improvement action is initiated on the basis of identified opportunities from many sources. Applying quality tools and techniques to analyse and solve them at all levels (with reference to Annex B)
- Analysis diagnoses tools introduces the range of quality tools available e.g. a Pareto diagram as shown on p.72. Providing advice on when to select an appropriate tool or technique

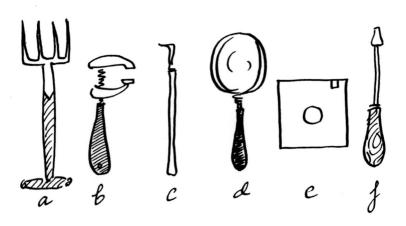

a   b   c   d   e   f

Annex A

This provides an example of a typical process of total quality management, a route to implementation:

1 Setting the policy and strategy of the organisation through:

- Establishing the mission of the corporate body
- Leadership and commitment of management and staff
- Divisional objectives as integrated elements of the corporate mission

2 Management of the organisation including:

- An effective organisational structure
- A management system implemented, audited and reviewed
- An information system providing key data
- An internal and external communication system

3 Improvement in the organisation with:

- Everyone contributing to the corporate mission
- Measurements of performance focused on customers
- Improvement objectives harmonised with the mission
- Improvement plans applied at all levels
- Monitoring and reviewing of the plans to ensure harmony and to check the gains made

Annex B

This provides an example of a systematic improvement process:

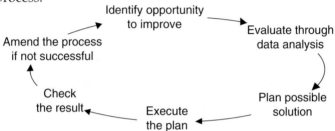

BS 7850: Part 2

This part of the Standard is designed to provide guidance on implementing TQM within an organisation. Describing the tools and techniques in a clearly illustrated manner, it is laid out as follows:

- A foreword
- A guide including:
  - Fundamental concepts
  - Managing for improving quality
  - A methodology for quality improvement
  - Supporting tools and techniques
- Annex A supporting tools and techniques

The *foreword* follows the approach in Part 1 and describes the objective of this part in describing the tools for use in continuous improvement.

The guide
The *introduction* emphasises that the purpose of implementing TQM is to improve quality continuously throughout the organisation. Motivated by an understanding that everything can be done:

- More effectively – giving improved results
- More efficiently – reducing the effort or resources required

The consequential benefits apply to the whole organisation.

The *scope* (1.0) confirms that this document covers guidance to implementing continuous quality improvement.

The *references* (2.0) include the normative reference to BS 4778: Quality Vocabulary, and the informative reference to part 1 of this standard.

The *definitions* (3.0), as well as referring to BS 4778 also include:

Process	Quality improvement
Quality losses	Corrective action
Preventive action	

The *fundamental concepts clause* (4.0) is in three sections described below.

1   The principles of quality improvement specifies how:

- Quality is defined by the customer
- Quality is fixed by the effectiveness and efficiency of the processes
- If you improve the process, you improve the quality
- Process improvement is continuous
- Improvement should be proactive
- Corrective action addresses existing problems
- Preventive action avoids problems

2   The environment for quality improvement schedules other factors important in quality improvement:

- Management responsibility and leadership by example, dedication, teamwork and empowerment
- New values, attitudes and behaviours need to be developed that are customer focused, involving everyone with open communications
- Quality improvement goals must be set that are customer focused and must be integrated into the business needs
- Communications and teamwork should be encouraged to remove barriers to improvement
- Recognition should follow the focus on quality improvement
- Education and training will be applied throughout the organisation

3   Quality losses can occur throughout the processes and provide the starting point for improvement. Even if intangible to begin with, these small gains can have significant impact.

Managing for quality improvement (5.0) covers the general application of techniques described in Annex A. It confirms that to be fully beneficial the focus must include:

1 Organising for quality improvement:

- Establishing vertical responsibilities, mission, ownership and spans of control
- Establishing horizontal responsibilities, customer and supplier relationships
- Establishing methods to formulate policies, strategies, resources and team coordination

2 Planning for quality improvement:

- Setting quality improvement goals and plans focused on important quality losses and new opportunities
- Involving all the staff, customers and suppliers
- Integrating projects and checking progress
- Involving a wide range of sources of data

3 Measuring quality improvement through an objective data-based system at every level. Identifying quality losses through:

- Customer satisfaction surveys or complaints Pnalysis
- Process costs of scrap, rework or inventories
- Social attitudes and issues e.g. employee satisfaction or environmental performance

A *methodology for quality improvement* (6.0), defines the steps to be taken involving the whole organisation when improvement projects are established, including:

- Initiating quality improvement projects to identify the need, scope, leader, team, resources and timetable
- Investigating possible areas for improvement to increase the understanding of the problem through data collection and analysis
- Establishing cause and effect relationships using the data to identify root causes, testing to validate conclusions
- Taking improvement action, testing possible solutions, pros and cons, before committing to action
- Confirming improvement after action, rechecking to ensure the problem has been solved
- Sustaining the gain by integrating the change into the business procedures
- Continuing the improvement by resetting objectives and targets

Supporting tools and techniques (7.0) refers to the detailed exploration of them in Annex A and confirms that:

- Successful quality improvement projects use these tools
- Decisions should be focused on numeric data
- Some empirical decisions are OK
- All staff should be trained in these tools and their application

Annex A

This describes and illustrates each of the common tools in detail, covering the following:

A.1 Data collection form   A method of systematically gathering data to provide a clear picture of the facts.

A.2 Affinity diagram   Used to organise a large number of ideas or issues to form a picture.

A.3 Benchmarking   Bridging our activities to recognised leaders to identify improvement opportunities.

A.4 Brainstorming   Tapping creative thinking in a team to identify QIP opportunities or solutions.

A.5 Cause and effect (fishbone) diagram   Analysis of relationships to assess possible causes of defects.

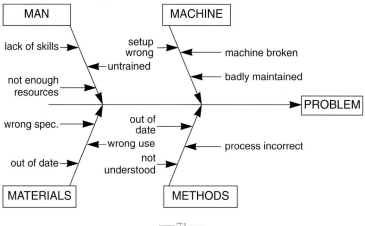

A.6 Flowchart   Displays a process pictorially for improved understanding.

A.7 Tree diagram   Displays logical relationships of elements to identify root causes.

A.8 Control charts   Monitor performance of a process against a statistical background to help set and assess improvement actions.

A.9 Histograms   Display of data to show variables against a common background.

A.10 Pareto diagram   Display of data ranking significant factors in priority order.

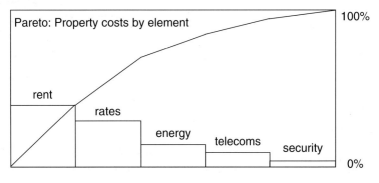

A.11 Scatter diagram   Graphical technique for assessing data to establish a relationship.

Summary

BS 7850 is a two-part guide to total quality management. Part 1 provides a guide to TQM principles indicating that leadership and commitment are key to unlocking the fundamental concepts. Part 2 provides a guide to quality improvement methods.

Planning implementation

Over the last three days we have looked in detail at quality management standard requirements and guidelines BS 5750, BS 7750 and BS 7850. Each of these standards provide some guidance on how to go about moving an organisation towards compliance with the standards. Today we will explore the common factors contained in these guides:

- Leadership and commitment
- Establishing a strategy
- Establishing the baseline
- Setting out the action plan
- Carrying out the action plan
- Measuring progress
- Maintaining the momentum

I'VE PLENTY OF LEADERSHIP AND COMMITMENT. I WAS ON THE MOBILE PHONE THIS MORNING TELLING PEOPLE WHAT TO DO!

Leadership and commitment

All the standards demonstrate that, as management own the business systems, leadership from the top of the organisation is essential because:

- Quality is a *management* issue
- Critical to success is time commitment, guided by *managers*
- Everyone will be effected, and everyone is *managed*
- The organisation will need to *change,*
- Change is the responsibility of *management*
- The key to continuous improvement is process *management*
- Quality improvement activities must be measured, controlled and *managed*

Setting our sights on complying with quality management standards is a project and like all projects it must be defined in a systematic and formal way.

Unlike most projects however, this one has no specific end, although we must set key milestones along the way to provide goals and to confirm progress. It is the start of a never-ending journey.

The milestones
These might be expressed as, 'Implement a quality system to meet the requirements of BS 5750 by March 1995 in our Cleanhome site.' Or, 'Include assessment against BS 7750 in our audit programme for 1995 with a view to establishing an action plan for compliance by 1996.' Or, 'Use TQM principles and concepts to reduce waste by xx to yy by April

1995 and improve customer satisfaction from xx% to yy% by May 1995.'

These specific goals must be agreed at executive level, using data from whatever sources are relevant to help in the setting of achievable but challenging objectives. Information sources may include:

- Cost of quality
- Customer complaints or surveys
- Legislation changes or breaches
- Staff suggestions/opinions
- Competition/financial results

Establishing a strategy

When the goal is set and the milestones along the way identified, the route map will resemble a continuous improvement loop:

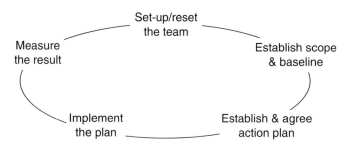

Executive management must ensure that the goal is communicated early on, and regular progress reviews and updates follow as the plan is implemented. To ensure this is done, we need to identify an executive manager with specific responsibility for compliance with the standards.

Setting up the team
As well as an executive owner, a large organisation may require a project manager dedicated to the task. With relevant technical skills in business and project management, he/she will be competent in leadership, communications and attention to detail.

The team will need to be drawn from every part of the organisation to ensure the programme reaches everywhere.

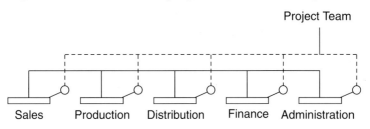

Defining the roles
Each member of the team has a role to play in the project, so each should be given a description of that role for inclusion in the performance planning activities.

The executive owner will lead the team, and provide the link to executive management and resources. The project manager will implement the programme through the team, establish the operational plan and report on progress. The departmental representatives will coordinate department activities, modifying the project to meet departmental needs.

Each member of the organisation has a role to play in the project, and each should be given a description of that role for inclusion in the performance planning activities.

Executive management should lead by example, commit resources and visibly track progress. Management should support the executive drive, lead their own team, allocate resources, and implement the changes. Staff should attend training, apply the principles, and participate.

Scope
The team needs to operate within a defined project scope to agree what will, and importantly, what will not be part of the project.

The scope may be limited to a site or subdivision of the organisation. It might limit the extent of the work, stopping short of third party certification or public reporting of environmental performance.

Given the scope, the team can identify the target action plan and the resources needed. These must be in balance with the schedule to ensure a success.

Establishing the baseline

Critical to success is the knowledge of the starting point to maximise the use of the skills and knowledge available:

- What is our current cost of quality?
- Who has had what relevant training?
- What procedures are currently documented?
- What do our competitors or best of breed do?
- What do customers think?
- What is our accident, incident or defect rate?
- Where are our risks for future success?
- What do our staff think?

This baseline will provide information to ensure that resources are focused on the key action areas.

Setting out the action plan

A step-by-step programme is required if we are to have
confidence in achieving the goal. The plan will show a
number of activities taking place over time, related to the
baseline and the milestones set for the team.

Quality Standards awareness
Quality Standards implementation
Process definition/improvement
Assessment and compliance
Continuous improvement

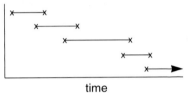

time

Carrying out the action plan

Each function, from management to the shop floor will
spend time:

- Learning about quality principles, tools and
  techniques
- Examining their own purpose, mission, goals and
  objectives
- Reviewing current activities, processes and
  measurements
- Revising the structure, systems and performance
  goals in the light of that information
- Establishing an initial quality improvement
  programme

The result of these actions is a proliferation of quality
improvement projects within a structured programme.
These might entail overhauling, simplifying and adding
new processes to suit the redefined business objectives.
These new activities may include:

- Process analysis and ownership charts
- Serviced level agreements between functions
- Focused quality improvement projects
- Quality circles
- Revised job description and organisation charts
- A demand for more training in other quality tools and techniques

Managers involved in the process can then identify the key areas on which to focus their energies.

Communication is key
We will tell people what is planned, then, as the plan rolls out, the focus will shift to coordinating the efforts taking place across the organisation.

Upward, downward and cross-department links will be reinforced as business processes are defined. The inputs and outputs between departments must be agreed and documented, leading to improved cohesion. New reporting mechanisms will include process measurements and improvement progress.

The degree of leadership interaction with the staff will increase as the changes are implemented. This is natural, and is an important part of the process, as there is a direct link between the success of quality initiatives and the commitment and interaction of leaders in the workplace.

Training provides the tools
We identified that further training demands will follow the roll-out programme, and these may include:

- Benchmarking skills
- Problem-solving techniques
- Process analysis and design skills
- Measurement and statistical analysis skills
- Job analysis, skill and competency needs assessment
- Personal skills in responding to change
- Technical skills in auditing, reporting and project management

Training in the new skills will not be enough, they must be applied in the workplace, and it is important that managers require, and reward, the application of these new skills.

Measuring progress

It will be necessary to measure progress diligently to ensure that the investment in time and effort is beneficial and demonstrably effective. Time and effort are often perceived as wasted in the early stages when very little evidence of improvements can be seen, and those reluctant to embark on the change process will then readily criticise the programme.

The milestones that formed part of the plan provide the first progress checks. In addition, we should look for:

- Awareness programme completed, how many staff involved?
- Implementation workshops, how many departments?
- Number of processes identified, owned and costed?
- Number of improvement activities started?
- Stages of the improvement projects reached?
- Internal audit achieved?
- External assessment passed?

In addition to the overview reporting, line managers can check in their own areas for:

- Job description reviewed and updated?
- Reorganisation plans progress?
- Benefits from process simplification recorded?
- Cross-functional agreements signed?

Executives will ultimately look at their own key measures:

- Product quality improvements, reduced waste, better delivery, fewer returns, more timeliness?
- Reduced cost of process activity, lower cost of quality, reduced resource cost or staff turnover?
- Higher customer satisfaction, market share or employee satisfaction?
- External visibility and market profile?

Maintaining the momentum

Initiating the project is just the start of the road to continuous improvement. Compliance with quality management standards is a new way of life for the organisation not a programme with an end date.

This leads to a constant seeking for improvement, which must be recognised by the internal culture of the organisation and its internal reward system. This culture is a shift towards rewarding those who grasp the process management issues, focus on the facts through practical measurement techniques, implement changes, and demonstrate improvement made.

In this environment, people will make mistakes and the management style has to be fault tolerant where errors occur in striving to improve. Ways to mitigate the impact of the errors along the way are:

- Establishing ownership unequivocally
- Undertaking risk assessment before significant changes
- Piloting changes in small areas
- Planning for identified failure possibilities
- Monitoring regularly and diligently
- Stopping identified failure quickly
- Trying again, learning from the failure

Summary

Today, we have looked at the key factors for implementing quality standards. The implementation is a continuous improvement process and must:

- Be management led
- Have a clear project structure
- Establish milestones along the way
- Measure progress diligently
- Communicate with, train and reward the people
- Continue through the failures

Achieving quality management standards

Today, we will review other activities related to quality management standards application:

- Self-assessment
- Internal audit
- External assessment
- Pitfalls and problems
- Investment and benefits

Self-assessment

On Friday, we identified the need to monitor progress towards applying quality management standards and obtaining the improvement benefits. A useful tool for many managers is something that would allow them to assess their own position: identifying areas that are well managed, those that need some attention, and those that require a more concentrated focus.

A self-assessment activity, if properly designed, will help identify those areas most in need of attention. Such a protocol can be tailored to the needs of our business. The characteristics of such a self-assessment programme are:

- Simplicity
- Low resource need
- Provide clear guidance
- Confidential

An example of the kind of questions is shown in the diagram overleaf, but we can design our own with a little thought about the issues we face.

Using self-assessments
These are best completed on a three- to six-monthly basis as an aid to understanding the position of the department, function or business process.

Do not be surprised to discover a very low score on the first attempt. The nature of using quality management standards as a yardstick to measure our own performance is the progression from identifying long-term problems and issues: 'We've always had that problem' through progress in reducing the areas that don't comply: 'We've always had that problem, but now I can see how we might tackle it' to putting in place the solution: 'We've always had that problem, but now we have a real solution to fix the root cause' and eventually confirming the compliant status: 'That used to be a problem, but now we are firmly in control.'

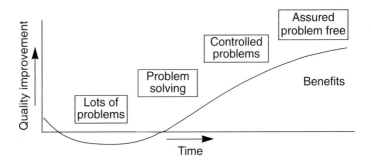

Self-assessment checklist

Not done at all   = **0**
Done but unsure of status = **1**
Satisfactory   = **2**
Performance good   = **3**
Excellent   = **4**

1 Is there an executive owner of the quality
    management standards compliance identified? **4 3 2 1 0**
2 Are our policies clearly defined and
    understood throughout the organisation? **4 3 2 1 0**
3 Have I clear communication routes inside
    and outside the organisation? **4 3 2 1 0**
4 Have I a written quality/environmental
    management system that meets the standard? **4 3 2 1 0**
5 Do my recognition and rewards programmes
    reflect my commitment to quality standards? **4 3 2 1 0**
6 Do the people in my organisation have
    documented roles and responsibilities? **4 3 2 1 0**
7 Are the staff skills and training needs
    identified and met? **4 3 2 1 0**
8 Do I have a process to understand my
    customer/interested parties requirements? **4 3 2 1 0**

9 Do I fully understand the environmental
effects of my activities and those that are
significant?   **4 3 2 1 0**

10 Have I set objectives and targets throughout
the organisation relevant to my policy,
customer needs and environmental effects?   **4 3 2 1 0**

11 Are all my business activities appropriately
planned and do the resources meet the needs?   **4 3 2 1 0**

12 Are my business processes documented
where lack of clarity could result in failure?   **4 3 2 1 0**

13 Do I measure and report the performance
of my processes to ensure they are effective?   **4 3 2 1 0**

14 Have I comprehensive information on
customer satisfaction, defects, waste and
energy use?   **4 3 2 1 0**

15 Have I well-established methods to correct
and prevent problems that are identified?   **4 3 2 1 0**

16 Are all my procedural documents
appropriately managed and maintained?   **4 3 2 1 0**

17 Do sufficient records and reporting
programmes exist to demonstrate compliance?   **4 3 2 1 0**

18 Do I have an appropriate audit programme
   in place to assure compliance?   **4 3 2 1 0**
19 Have I a follow-up programme to resolve
   issues identified in the audit?   **4 3 2 1 0**
20 Do I regularly review with executive
   management the status of my systems
   compliance?   **4 3 2 1 0**

Internal audit

The approach to an internal audit should be the same as for
protocols and procedures for an external assessment. As
well as ensuring compliance with confidence, this approach
familiarises the staff with the style of audit work – the 'Show
me?' approach to questioning.

New skills may be needed to ensure that the managers
understand the role of the audit programme to remove the
fear and resistance commonly associated with these
activities.

Audit procedures and protocols
These are laid down in ISO 10011: Quality Systems
Auditing, which is a three-part standard:

- ISO 10011-1: Auditing
- ISO 10011-2: Qualification Criteria for Auditors
- ISO 10011-3: Managing an Audit Programme

ISO 10011-1: Auditing   Provides guidelines for the basic
audit principles, criteria and practices covering:

- Establishing an audit process
- Planning quality system audits
- Carrying out the audit
- Documenting the audit results

ISO 10011-2: Qualification Criteria for Auditors   Gives guidance on the qualifications needed by auditors to carry out their roles effectively:

- Educational status and communication competencies
- Auditor training of applicable standards, assessment techniques and planning skills
- Experience in quality systems environments
- Personal attributes – objectivity, sensitivity, focused, consistent and balanced individuals
- Management skills
- Ongoing competency to be maintained

ISO 10011-3: Managing an Audit Programme   Provides guidance on the management of a programme:

- Organisational capability
- Quality management standards to audit against
- Staff qualifications
- Team profile and skill mix
- Audit performance monitoring
- Operational issues including:
  - resources
  - scheduling
  - reporting
  - corrective action follow-up
  - confidentiality
- Audit programme improvement
- Ethics

Use of these three guidelines will ensure competent and consistent quality management system audits that add value, highlighting areas of non-compliance for management action.

External assessments

The use of an outside organisation to carry out assessments and certification has grown from the need of customers to see more objective evidence of conformance.

In order to have confidence in the third party assessment bodies, the customer requires assurance of the capability and skill of the assessment body. This is provided by the National Accreditation Council for Certification Bodies (NACCB).

The NACCB was set up by the DTI to provided independent assessment of the capabilities of certification bodies through an accreditation process. Accredited certification bodies are given the right to display the NACCB mark alongside their own certification mark:

NATIONAL
ACCREDITATION
OF CERTIFICATION
BODIES

Registration Number

Pitfalls and problems

Many organisations report difficulties in implementing quality management standards, from the impact of the changes, to the perception of the 'bureaucratic' nature of the business processes established.

Experience has shown, however, that the most common causes of failure occur in three areas.

Commitment from the top
This is essential for success. Lack of dedication and commitment here will result in failure to implement the necessary changes throughout the organisation. It is important that senior managers practise the philosophy as well as encourage and lead others.

Consistency in approach
The initial stages usually uncover a multitude of problems, but there is no going back. This is not a 'flavour of the month' programme but a change in concept, style and

values throughout the organisation. The challenges uncovered must be addressed in a proactive and diligent manner. The functional elements of the business, from systems to structures, staff to strategies must reflect a dedication to the quality philosophy.

Capitalising on the gain

Like a new diet, benefits may quickly show, but without a change in life style, it is difficult to hold the gain. The new benefits could be lost in the next crisis or reorganisation. It is important, therefore, that the quality management standards compliance forms the backbone of the organisation, around which it can change and develop.

There should always be a process to review the 'contract' with the customer, but it can change as often as we want. There should always be a process to inspect and test products in production, but how and when is up to us.

The goal is to reach the stage where quality problems do not occur, and where managers know that this is due to the measurable effectiveness of the system.

Investment and benefits

There is an investment to be made to gain the benefits of the new approach, as with any new piece of plant or equipment.

The core investment in reorienting the organisation involves a considerable amount of 'people time', learning the new skills and transferring them into the organisation.

The net effect initially is negative, as a lot of time and effort goes in, with little improvement to show. Over time, however, the benefits in improved business performance begin to flow through and greatly repay the efforts, as measured 'cost of quality' falls:

Cost of quality is the measure we place on the wasted effort in the organisation due to failure in the internal processes and systems. This varies in organisations, but an accepted figure is around 20 per cent of turnover – that's right – up to one day per week per person could be wasted because our quality management is not right. Cost of quality is measured in:

Waste Failure where the product or serviced could not be used and is wasted; time and effort redoing things; lost customers, litigation, fines and other direct costs that flow from our mistakes.

Checking Appraisal to reduce the cost of waste: inspecting, testing, assessing costs, time and effort to indicate areas of failure.

Avoidance Prevention measures, risk analysis, planning activities and process re-engineering cost time and effort, but they are essential if waste is to be kept to a minimum.

Improved quality management systems have the effect of increasing the problem avoidance costs and decreasing the checking/appraisal, and ultimately waste/failure, costs:

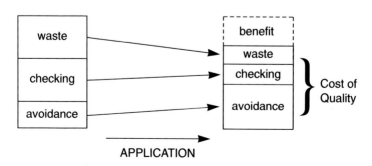

Summary

The application of quality management standards is a new way of life for many organisations and provides:

- A common benchmark against which to assess our management systems
- A systematic approach to improving our management performance and through that the organisation
- A vocabulary, tools and techniques that provide an opportunity to refocus our management effort
- An opportunity to develop new skills throughout the organisation
- A market-recognised standard of excellence to provide competitive advantage
- A reduction in bottom line operating costs through waste reduction
- An improvement in customer satisfaction leading to improved profitability
- An improvement in our legal and environmental performance and compliance
- Improved perceptions of our overall status with all our stakeholders
- A sense of achievement

The Successful Business in a Week series

Successful Appraisals in a Week
Successful Assertiveness in a Week
Successful Budgeting in a Week
Successful Business Writing in a Week
Successful Career Planning in a Week
Successful Computing for Business in a Week
Finance for Non-Financial Managers in a Week
Successful Interviewing in a Week
Understanding Just in Time in a Week
Successful Marketing in a Week
Successful Market Research in a Week
Successful Meetings in a Week
Successful Mentoring in a Week
Successful Motivation in a Week
Successful Presentation in a Week
Successful Project Management in a Week
Successful Public Relations in a Week
Successful Negotiating in a Week
Successful Selling in a Week
Successful Stress Management in a Week
Successful Time Management in a Week
Successful Training in a Week
Understanding Quality Management Standards in a Week
Understanding Total Quality Management in a Week
Doing Business in Europe